Dancing into Shadows and Light

Jocelyn Flojo

BookLeaf Publishing

India | USA | UK

Presentation by *BookLeaf Publishing*

Web: www.bookleafpub.com

E-mail: info@bookleafpub.com

ISBN: 9789360945466

First edition 2024

Time Slips

Time slips
Missed trips
And you have long gone.

Wedding bells
But no tales to tell
Those chimes were not ours to hear.

When silence becomes
The bearer of bad news
It's worse than a call (not received).

I thought that day
When you said you would stay
Was all the reassurance I would need.

But I was corrected
In advance of the rejections
The first time I saw you (and her) leave.

Supernova

Loin des yeux.
Loin de coeur.
Out of sight.
Out of mind.

But why does my heart grow fonder?
I have almost forgotten
Your eyes
Your smile
Your voice.
But a memory pushes forward.

I know it cannot be mutual.
Any thoughts of me, may have never even
existed.
But the spark in my heart
Flickers then flames
Trying to ignite
Without any kindling or tinder.

With no resolve
This may just evolve
And like an exploding star,
Supernova.

The Letter

A letter hidden between pages by Keats
Sometimes she forgets about it herself.
Written when she thought
She could be open
And share what she felt
But stopped when she knew it couldn't be real.
She told herself over again in time
So that the falseness overpowered the truth.
The words written were lies,
She convinced her mind.
But the beat of her heart knew better.
So the letter remains,
Folded edges,
Sharp and thin,
That it may just dissolve and tear on its own.
This is her hope…
As she can't let it go.

Law of Attraction

Laws of attraction fail me all the time.
Laws of distraction get in the way
The more we try to ignore and avoid
The more persistent it gets.
But there's no other choice.
Give in or give up.
Live or die…and even in death it may still exist.

Haunting us, until when?
Who's in charge?
Not my head, always my heart.
Is there a drug or remedy?
If there is — give it to me.
I'll be first in line —
Wait night and day —
Until I can make it go away.
The Law of Attraction — who wrote it?
Destroy it, so I can forget.

In My Head

Candid photos,
Only in my head.
I caught a glimpse of you
And saved the image once again.
Too scared to say anything,
Once again.
I'll imagine we've talked,
Only in my head,
And save that conversation
As false as it may be.
And when the day comes
When my thoughts become actual words,
I'll say things that make me awkward,
Not knowing what to say
And having so much I want to say.
In that moment my tongue becomes tangled
And all I can do is smile
And say "cool" or "nice" or "that's great" —
When it's none of the above.
Because what I feel
You'll never know or see
Because it's only in my head.

Late Night

Late night talks under starlit skies,
Reminisce about the past,
When we were lost
In our youth.
Now dreaming, planning, wishing
For a moment or more
Where dreams no longer lay dormant —
Now tangible, real and true.
A future in our eyes
Can be seen with the reflection of the moon's
light,
Gazing down upon us
Where romance is no longer hidden
Between the pages of a novel,
Or a journal,
But here in the air
Between two souls.
Surrounding us now
No longer lost in the past,
Or forgotten in the future,
We breathe it in
At last.

A Thought of You

I read a poem the other day
That reminded me of you.
It spoke of laughter in a lover's eyes
The joyful promise that brings hope in one's
heart
The soft touch and embrace that lasts
Longingly between two loves.
All just a thought
For you and I now
As days, weeks, months
Have separated us and continues on.
Our mornings no longer the same
With a thought or wonder
Of what the other is doing,
Or a night that is preceded by "good" is shared.
We wonder if it ever happened at all.
It's easier to think it was imagined or dreamed
—

Another lifetime maybe.
The past? The future?
No longer now.

Bliss

A heavy heart no longer weighs me down.
I have freed myself
From the external thoughts that pull
And prohibit my liberation.
Focusing on my own light and energy
Breathed into me from my faith
Finding joy internally now —
In myself and for myself.
Not being selfish
But selfless for myself — at last.
Judgement may come
Where I will dismiss each one.
Trusting myself,
My intuition,
My God —
Guiding me to move forward
Where blessings may come —
Relying on no one
But me.
Bliss becomes abundant.

Bloom

Unexpected connections,
A look that turns into a stare
Until one notices
And quickly looks away.
"Was it obvious?" A question asked in silence.
"It is." An answer unknown.
Moving closer just to be near
But no need to say a word.
A slight touch as a pass takes place,
A reach nearby for something out of reach,
Until a laugh is shared
And introductions are made.
A story and an anecdote to break the ice
And the look is shared again, and received,
With no more need to turn away.
A friendship will bloom
And friendships will turn to love once more.

Breathe

Inhale to exhale
And breathe free
To release —
The thoughts,
The pain.
But memories will remain —
For now.
Until then I'll take these deep breaths,
Though they hurt,
My heart feels the shame
For being so naïve,
So innocent.
It floats too easily
When romance is the temptation—
A fleeting fantasy and feeling.
She escapes the mind too easily
And regrets it because it always ends the same.
So breathe in
And breathe out
And breathe on.
One day this too will be kept hidden,
And locked away,
Until its memory no longer remains.

Trophies

I hear your voice,
I hear you laugh,
And it resonates so clear.
Even within a crowd
I can recognize you,
Even when I don't look or search.
I miss it all —
Though you don't know.
You won't know.
My will and pride will not allow it.
I'll just remember us — where it once was —
In a time capsule
Buried within me.
As you move on
Pretending you don't know me,
Or recognize me;
Apathy is natural for you.
You like to win
And so you have.
My defeat and sadness are your trophies.
Keep them high on a shelf,
Behind glass,
As you do now.

Your Presence

I dreamt of you
Again last night.
You were laughing,
Smiling,
Happy to be with me.
When I awoke
And found that it wasn't real,
The euphoria still remained,
Where I smiled throughout the day.
Your presence —
Your touch,
Your scent,
Your spirit,
Escaped my dreams
To live with me here in my existence.
I'll hold on to it — close —
And pray that it doesn't leave me,
Although you have.
Still grateful to have had you — even briefly —
A memory or dream,
I'll take it and treasure it,
For that's all I have left of you now.

Blinded by Moonlight

Blinded by moonlight
Is that possible?
My eyes fixated, dilated,
Drawn to its spherical glow.
And I wonder
If you see it too
Where you are
Looking into the night
Gazing at the sky,
Along with me,
But not with me —
Far away, miles away —
Only by distance
But not by thought.
I wish I could pull in the moon,
And pull you in too.
Tethered, you are to it,
From another angle,
Another time,
To bring you closer.
But no worries.
Because the moon's light,
We're staring at it now,
Taking in its beauty together.

Happy to Meet You

Hello, I am so happy to meet you.
How do you do?
A moment so long ago.
And here we are once more.

I've been waiting for the moment
When the stars aligned
And we would see one another once again.
Have you been well?
What have you been up to?
Have you thought of me at all
While I've been away?

I've thought of you often —
More than I care to share.
So I won't let you know.
I'll just smile, give you a wave,
And a warm embrace.

As time and place pushed between us two
We have slowly become more like strangers
Than friends,
Than lovers,
Once upon that time.

You used to hold me in the middle of the night
—

In the dark
When the night air breezed through the crack of
a window
And left goosebumps and chills.
Though we knew they were from our feelings
felt.
When the sun would hide from the moon,
As its light would cascade your face —
The only part of you I could see.

Eyes shut as you dreamed.
And when I dreamed
It was always of you.
Always happy when I would awaken
And see you there beside me still.

No longer the case,
But you still linger in my unconscious mind
In the middle of dark nights.

Hello, I am so happy to see you again.
"You look well, " you tell me now.
The façade has been practiced,
Knowing a day like this may come.
"Thank you, you too," I reply.
A brief hug once more,
As we begin to move the opposite way.

Slow Moving Tides

Waves crashing yet I hear nothing —
So calm and peaceful still,
Silent and immovable.
The horizon with the sun piercing through the clouds
On the deep blue canvas
Not wanting to leave.
This space so far,
Thousands of miles away
From what I know —
From familiarity
The routine, the mundane
The predictable.

I don't know if this is real,
A paradise that I am existing in now
Where the shoreline's elevations transition
From high to low —
Not only the tides
But the terrain.
The people move wistfully through,
Unknowing and unaware
How someone like me,
So far removed into this new world,
Does not take it for granted —

Even with the random sounds of vehicles
Moving about in the background.

My departure just days away
And I'm already saddened by it.
Looking through dates in the calendar
Timing it just right —
Perfectly,
So that I may visit again.

Breathing in the breeze,
Looking out in the limitless ocean
Grasping for moments to last longer.
As the seconds go on pause here,
Time lasts longer in this place,
Leaving a piece of me each time I take my
breath
Hoping for a time, a moment
When I can come back again.

The Storm

Palm leaves strewn about
As the rain and wind rush through
Trying to catch a breath in between
Gasping for air
Closing my eyes shut
Trying to keep the drops from flooding my
vision
This temporary storm
Or so they say
Will pass through quickly
Just a moment more
Trying to find shelter in the middle of the block
I duck behind a skewed doorframe
Between one empty space and another
Only to get a brief respite
From this ruthless torrent
Beating me down with the cold and the wet
Unprepared (unusual for me)
As I await for the storm to subside
It stops as quickly as it began
I expose myself to the elements again
And continue my journey on
Taking each step closer to the warmth
Of my shelter
My home

Friday Night Seaside

Reflections jagged and broken
Staggered about with each wave of the ocean
Birds flying far above
Then glide gracefully past me
As if to guide my way
Showing me where the sun will settle in
This evening and the next

As my steps and stride
Move consistently ahead
As if marching to the the beat of the waves
Crashing along the shore
It takes me closer to the sounds
Of laughter
Of chatter
Of storefronts selling local wares
And fresh caught seafood,
Married with the smell of cinnamon and sugar
from
Fudge and ice cream,
Churros and almonds,
My palate is enticed.

The rhythm of the drum and the strum of guitars
near

A local band is already playing
Familiar choruses and melodies
As sing alongs from the crowd add to the
jubilation
Another evening in the small seaside town
Is my home away from home

The Moonlit Path

Moon so brightly
Lighting the path
Dogs with their owners stroll past
Silently and steadfast
As this night
Cool but just right
As the steps increase
And the pace quickens
With my heart beating faster
As the minutes pass
The clear sky
Where I begin to count the stars
Until it begins to look limitless
I gaze to my left
To see a couple embrace
As their heads touch
To steal a secret kiss
Myself forgetting what that feels like
Not understanding why
I feel just fine
Knowing that my days have been blessed
With the confidence of being happy
In my independence
My success in reaching goals
Internally within myself

I soon reach the invisible finish line
Where I take a deep breath
And see how far I have come

The Tides of Life Move Slowly

The tides of life move slowly
Never the same as they approach and leave
The shores where we meet
At once time seems to stand still
As we patiently wait for moments
Held near to our souls
While at the same time
Swiftly we have changed
Grown and aged
But it's just like we only met yesterday
As young kids
In a small town
Not even knowing that our future would look
like as it does now
Finding one another again
After so many years
We walk together
Side by side
Reconnecting and growing
A loving friendship to hold dear

Signs and Symbols

Symbols surround us
As the minutes pass throughout the day
Lucky numbers noticed on buildings and clocks
Names displayed on signs that we never saw
before
Even characters and animals that have special
meaning
Seem to appear in unlikely places

As we traverse through the path we've walked a
night before
Butterflies flutter past in front of us and then
above
Guiding and guarding
A myriad of colors and types
Surprising us from branches and bushes
Billowing from either side
I giggle and gasp with joy at their sight
Hoping they have a secret meaning
Just as the other signs collected
In invisible pockets within my mind
Until the heart captures them
And asks for more

Fierce Moon

Fine mists from the ocean spray
As waves crash fiercely
Onto cragged rocks and boulders
Abandoned on the shore
By God's hands
Hundreds or thousands of years before
Evening's tranquility is lost now
By the moon's forceful tide
As she bears down from above
Orchestrating a symphony from
Cacophony of the seaside sounds
Cold air commences
As the sun is now fully dormant
Its slumber cannot be disturbed
Even with the strength of nature
Taking over this coast
Her time to rise will come
When it is time
But that is not now
For the moon has taken over
Encompassing this winter's night
Just be still
And let her work be done